To A Wonderful Student:

All boys love Easter
bunnies, chocolate, egg hunts, and
a basket full of wonderful things!

I hope Easter is egg-citing...
filled with fun and adventure for
a WONDERFUL STUDENT!

A boy as special as you
should get your favorite
goodies from the Easter bunny!

Here's wishing the Easter Bunny brings you the best and most colorful eggs!

HOP! HOP! HOP! The Easter Bunny is on his way to make sure you have plenty of sweet treats!

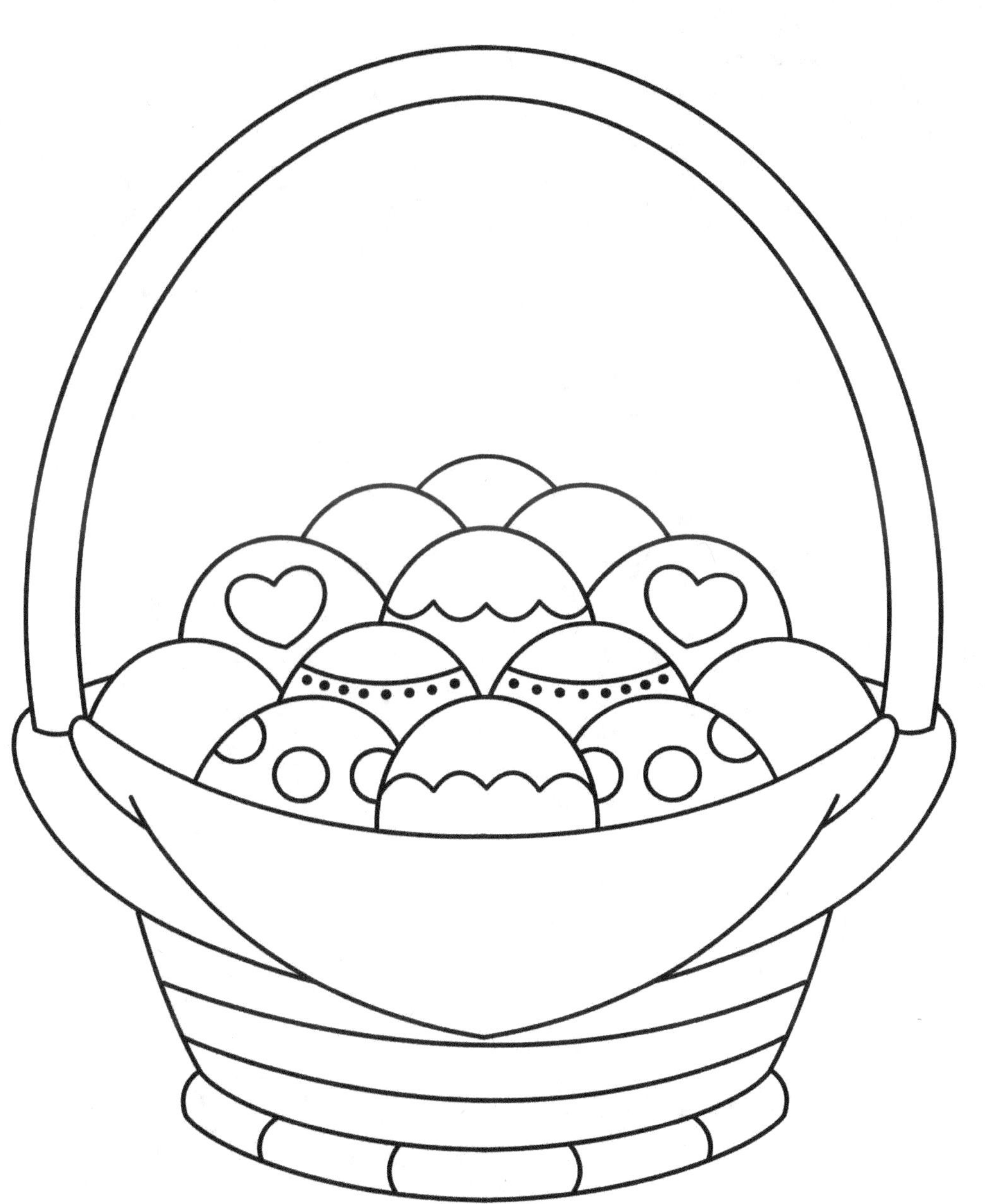

Wishing you a wonderful time as you celebrate Easter with family & friends!

One of the best things about Easter is...
all of the chocolate eggs
boys get to eat!

The Easter Bunny told me that you are an EGG-STRA WONDERFUL STUDENT!

There is no other boy in the world that deserves more fun than you this Easter!

Have a fantastic Easter with plenty of chirping chickens & fluffy bunnies!

Good luck this year on your
Easter egg hunt!

Happy Easter
To A Wonderful Student!
(Coloring Card)
(Personalized Card) Easter Messages,
Wishes, & Greetings for Children!

May you have a wonderful
holiday and your basket is filled with
lots of holiday things.

www.ingramcontent.com/pod-product-compliance
Lightning Source LLC
Chambersburg PA
CBHW051931250726
48659CB00002B/957